DINER
Cookbook

Publications International, Ltd.

Pictured on the front cover *(left to right):* Easy Patty Melt *(page 56)* and Strawberry Shake *(page 120).*
Pictured on the back cover *(top to bottom):* French Toast with Orange Butter *(page 14),* Cheeseburger Chowder *(page 26)* and Classic Apple Pie *(page 116).*

ISBN-13: 978-1-60553-214-1
ISBN-10: 1-60553-214-2

Library of Congress Control Number: 2009936101

Manufactured in China.

8 7 6 5 4 3 2 1

Microwave Cooking: Microwave ovens vary in wattage. Use the cooking times as guidelines and check for doneness before adding more time.

Preparation/Cooking Times: Preparation times are based on the approximate amount of time required to assemble the recipe before cooking, baking, chilling or serving. These times include preparation steps such as measuring, chopping and mixing. The fact that some preparations and cooking can be done simultaneously is taken into account. Preparation of optional ingredients and serving suggestions is not included.

Publications International, Ltd.

TABLE OF CONTENTS

Corned Beef Hash

2 large russet potatoes, cut into ½-inch cubes
½ teaspoon salt
¼ teaspoon black pepper
¼ cup (½ stick) butter
1 large onion, chopped
½ pound corned beef, finely chopped
1 tablespoon prepared horseradish
¼ cup whipping cream (optional)
4 eggs

1. Place potatoes in large skillet. Cover potatoes with water. Bring to a boil over high heat. Reduce heat to low; simmer 6 minutes. (Potatoes will be firm.) Drain potatoes in colander; sprinkle with salt and pepper.

2. Melt butter in skillet; add onion. Cook and stir over medium-high heat 5 minutes. Stir in corned beef, horseradish and potatoes; mix well. Press down mixture with spatula to flatten.

3. Reduce heat to low. Drizzle cream evenly over mixture, if desired. Cook 10 to 15 minutes. Turn with spatula; pat down and cook 10 to 15 minutes or until browned.

4. Meanwhile, poach eggs. Serve hash topped with eggs.

Makes 4 servings

Apple Pecan Pastries

½ of a 17.3-ounce package PEPPERIDGE FARM® Puff Pastry Sheets
    (1 sheet)
1 cup packed brown sugar
½ cup all-purpose flour
1 teaspoon ground cinnamon
⅛ teaspoon ground nutmeg
2 cups peeled, diced Granny Smith apples
1 cup chopped pecans
1 tablespoon cold butter, cut into pieces
    Confectioners' sugar

1. Thaw the pastry sheet at room temperature for 40 minutes or until it's easy to handle. Heat the oven to 375°F. Lightly grease a baking sheet.

2. Stir the brown sugar, flour, cinnamon and nutmeg in a medium bowl. Add the apples, pecans and butter and toss to coat.

3. Unfold the pastry sheet on a lightly floured surface. Roll the pastry sheet into a 15×10-inch rectangle. Brush the pastry sheet with water. With the long side facing you, spoon the apple mixture on the pastry to within 2 inches of the long sides and to the edge of the short sides. Starting at a long side, roll up like a jelly roll. Cut the pastry roll into 12 (1¼-inch) slices. Place the slices 2 inches apart on the baking sheet.

4. Bake for 15 minutes or until the pastries are golden. Remove the pastries from the baking sheet and cool on a wire rack. Sprinkle with the confectioners' sugar.   *Makes 12 pieces*

Kitchen Tip: You can substitute chopped walnuts for the pecans if you like.

Thaw Time: 40 minutes • Prep Time: 20 minutes • Bake Time: 15 minutes

Banana-Nut Buttermilk Waffles

¾ cup walnuts or pecans
2 cups all-purpose flour
¼ cup sugar
2 teaspoons baking powder
1 teaspoon salt
2 eggs, separated
2 cups buttermilk
2 very ripe bananas, mashed (about 1 cup)
¼ cup (½ stick) butter, melted
1 teaspoon vanilla
    Syrup and banana slices
    Additional walnuts (optional)

1. Toast walnuts in medium nonstick skillet over medium heat 5 to 8 minutes or until fragrant, stirring frequently. Transfer to plate to cool; chop and set aside.

2. Preheat waffle iron according to manufacturer's directions.

3. Meanwhile, combine flour, sugar, baking powder and salt in large bowl. Beat egg yolks in medium bowl. Add buttermilk, mashed bananas, butter, vanilla and walnuts; mix well. Stir buttermilk mixture into flour mixture just until moistened.

4. Beat egg whites in separate medium bowl with electric mixer at high speed until stiff but not dry. Fold egg whites into batter.

5. Pour ¾ cup batter into waffle iron; bake 4 to 6 minutes or until golden. Serve with syrup and banana slices. Garnish with additional walnuts.
                                                    Makes 4 servings

Garlic Cheddar Grits

2 tablespoons butter
2 cloves garlic, minced
4 cups (32 ounces) low-sodium chicken broth*
1 cup uncooked grits (not instant)
2 cups (8 ounces) shredded sharp Cheddar cheese, plus more for
    topping
2 eggs
¼ to ½ teaspoon salt
    Hot pepper sauce or ground red pepper

*This amount of broth will produce creamy grits. For a firmer texture, reduce broth to 3½ cups.

1. Melt butter in large saucepan over medium-high heat. Add garlic; cook and stir 30 seconds. Add broth; bring to a boil over high heat. Stir in grits; reduce heat. Cover; simmer 15 minutes or until creamy, stirring occasionally.

2. Meanwhile, preheat oven to 375°F. Lightly grease 1½-quart casserole or 9-inch deep-dish pie plate.

3. Remove grits from heat; stir in cheese until melted. Beat eggs in small bowl until thick and pale yellow. Stir 1 spoonful of grits into eggs until well blended. Fold egg mixture into remaining grits. Season to taste with salt and hot pepper sauce. Spoon into prepared casserole.

4. Bake 40 to 45 minutes or until golden brown and center is set. Top with additional cheese, if desired.   *Makes 8 servings*

Quick Cinnamon Sticky Buns

1 cup packed light brown sugar, divided
10 tablespoons butter, softened and divided
1 package (16 ounces) hot roll mix
2 tablespoons granulated sugar
1 cup hot water (120° to 130°F)
1 egg
1⅔ cups (10-ounce package) HERSHEY'S Cinnamon Chips

1. Lightly grease two 9-inch round baking pans. Combine ½ cup brown sugar and 4 tablespoons softened butter in small bowl until smooth; spread half of mixture evenly on bottom of prepared pans. Set aside.

2. Combine contents of hot roll mix package, including yeast packet, and granulated sugar in large bowl. Using spoon, stir in water, 2 tablespoons butter and egg until dough pulls away from sides of bowl. Turn dough onto lightly floured surface. With lightly floured hands, shape into ball. Knead 5 minutes or until smooth, using additional flour if necessary.

3. To shape: Using lightly floured rolling pin, roll into 15×12-inch rectangle. Spread with remaining 4 tablespoons butter. Sprinkle with remaining ½ cup brown sugar and cinnamon chips, pressing lightly into dough. Starting with 12-inch side, roll tightly as for jelly roll; seal edges.

4. Cut into 1-inch-wide slices with floured knife. Arrange 6 slices, cut sides down, in each prepared pan. Cover with towel; let rise in warm place until doubled, about 30 minutes.

5. Heat oven to 350°F. Uncover rolls. Bake 25 to 30 minutes or until golden brown. Cool 2 minutes in pans; with knife, loosen around edges of pans. Invert onto serving plates. Serve warm or at room temperature.

Makes 12 cinnamon buns

Steak Hash

2 tablespoons vegetable oil
1 green bell pepper, chopped
½ medium onion, chopped
2 or 3 medium russet potatoes (about 1 pound), cooked and cut into
  bite-size pieces
½ pound cooked steak or roast beef, cut into 1-inch pieces
  Salt and black pepper
¼ cup (1 ounce) shredded Monterey Jack cheese
4 eggs

1. Heat oil in large skillet over medium heat. Add bell pepper and onion; cook and stir until crisp-tender. Stir in potatoes; reduce heat to low. Cover and cook, stirring occasionally, about 10 minutes or until potatoes are heated through.

2. Stir in steak; season with salt and pepper. Sprinkle with cheese. Cover; cook 5 minutes or until steak is heated through and cheese is melted.

3. Meanwhile, poach eggs. Top each serving of hash with egg.

Makes 4 servings

Hash is a delicious way to use leftovers. Next time you bake potatoes for dinner, add a few extras to the oven. Keep them in the refrigerator overnight and use them for hash the next morning. There's no need to peel potatoes for hash. The peel is nutritious and adds texture and flavor to the dish.

French Toast with Orange Butter

⅓ cup whipped butter, softened
2 tablespoons orange marmalade
2 teaspoons honey
4 eggs, beaten
½ cup milk
2 tablespoons granulated sugar
1 teaspoon ground cinnamon
1 teaspoon vanilla
¼ teaspoon ground nutmeg
8 ounces French bread, cut diagonally into 8 slices
2 tablespoons vegetable oil
   Powdered sugar (optional)

1. Blend butter, marmalade and honey in small bowl; set aside.

2. Whisk together eggs, milk, granulated sugar, cinnamon, vanilla and nutmeg in medium bowl. Dip bread slices into egg mixture. Place on large platter.

3. Heat 1 tablespoon oil in large skillet over medium heat. Add bread in single layer; cook 3 minutes per side or until golden. Repeat with remaining bread, adding additional oil as needed.

4. Sprinkle with powdered sugar, if desired, and serve with orange butter.
Makes 4 servings

Ham and Vegetable Omelet

Nonstick cooking spray
½ cup diced ham
1 small onion, diced
1 medium green or red bell pepper, diced
2 cloves garlic, minced
6 eggs, beaten
Salt and black pepper
½ cup (2 ounces) shredded Colby cheese, divided
1 medium tomato, chopped
Hot pepper sauce (optional)

1. Spray 12-inch nonstick skillet with cooking spray; heat over medium-high heat. Add ham, onion, bell pepper and garlic; cook and stir 5 minutes or until vegetables are crisp-tender. Transfer mixture to large bowl.

2. Pour eggs into skillet; season with salt and black pepper. Cook over medium-high heat 2 minutes or until bottom is set, lifting edge with spatula to allow uncooked portion to flow underneath. Reduce heat to medium-low. Cover; cook 4 minutes or until top is set.

3. Gently slide omelet onto large serving plate; spoon ham mixture down center. Sprinkle with ¼ cup cheese. Fold omelet over ham mixture. Sprinkle with remaining ¼ cup cheese and tomato. Serve with hot pepper sauce, if desired.   *Makes 4 servings*

Easy Raspberry-Peach Danish

1 loaf (about 16 ounces) frozen white bread dough, thawed
1/3 cup raspberry fruit spread
1 can (16 ounces) sliced peaches in juice, drained and chopped
1 egg white, beaten (optional)
1/2 cup powdered sugar
2 to 3 teaspoons orange juice
1/4 cup chopped pecans, toasted*

Spread nuts in shallow baking pan. Bake in preheated 350°F oven 5 minutes or until fragrant, stirring occasionally.

1. Spray 2 baking sheets with nonstick cooking spray.

2. Place dough on lightly floured surface; cut in half. Roll each half into 12×7-inch rectangle. Place 1 rectangle on each prepared baking sheet.

3. Spread half of raspberry spread over center third of each dough rectangle. Sprinkle peaches over raspberry spread. Make 2-inch long cuts from edges towards filling on long sides of each dough rectangle at 1-inch intervals. Fold strips of dough over filling. Cover; let rise in warm place about 1 hour or until nearly doubled in size.

4. Preheat oven to 350°F. Bake 15 to 20 minutes or until golden. For a deeper golden color, lightly brush egg white over tops of Danish during last 5 minutes of baking. Remove Danish to wire rack; cool slightly.

5. Combine powdered sugar and enough orange juice in small bowl to make pourable glaze. Drizzle over Danish. Sprinkle with pecans.

Makes 32 servings

Prep Time: 15 minutes • **Rising Time:** 1 hour • **Bake Time:** 15 to 20 minutes

Cheddar Broccoli Frittata

6 eggs, beaten
1 can (10¾ ounces) CAMPBELL'S® Condensed Broccoli Cheese or
    98% Fat Free Broccoli Cheese Soup
¼ cup milk
⅛ teaspoon ground black pepper
1 tablespoon butter or margarine
2 cups sliced mushrooms (about 6 ounces)
1 large onion, chopped (about 1 cup)
1 small zucchini, sliced (about 1 cup)
¼ cup shredded Cheddar cheese (1 ounce)
1 green onion, chopped (about 2 tablespoons)

1. Mix eggs, soup, milk and black pepper.

2. Heat butter in large ovenproof nonstick skillet over medium heat. Add mushrooms, onion and zucchini and cook until tender. Add soup mixture. Cook over medium-low heat 8 minutes or until eggs are set but still moist.

3. Sprinkle cheese over egg mixture.

4. Broil 4 inches from heat 2 minutes or until golden brown. Sprinkle with green onion. Cut into wedges.   *Makes 4 servings*

Tip: To make skillet ovenproof, wrap handle in aluminum foil.

Prep Time: 10 minutes • **Cook Time:** 15 minutes

Jumbo Streusel-Topped Raspberry Muffins

2¼ cups all-purpose flour, divided
¼ cup packed brown sugar
2 tablespoons cold butter
¾ cup granulated sugar
2 teaspoons baking powder
½ teaspoon baking soda
½ teaspoon salt
½ teaspoon grated lemon peel
¾ cup plus 2 tablespoons milk
⅓ cup butter, melted
1 egg, beaten
2 cups fresh or frozen raspberries (do not thaw)

1. Preheat oven to 350°F. Grease 6 jumbo (3½-inch) muffin cups.

2. For topping, combine ¼ cup flour and brown sugar in small bowl. Cut in cold butter with pastry blender or two knives until mixture forms coarse crumbs.

3. Reserve ¼ cup flour in medium bowl. Combine remaining 1¾ cups flour, granulated sugar, baking powder, baking soda, salt and lemon peel in medium bowl. Combine milk, melted butter and egg in small bowl.

4. Add milk mixture to flour mixture; stir until almost blended. Toss raspberries with reserved flour just until coated; gently fold raspberries into muffin batter. Spoon batter into prepared muffin cups, filling three-fourths full. Sprinkle with topping.

5. Bake 25 to 30 minutes or until toothpick inserted into centers comes out clean. Cool in pan 2 minutes; remove to wire rack. Serve warm or at room temperature.   *Makes 6 jumbo muffins*

Variation: For smaller muffins, spoon batter into 12 standard (2½-inch) greased or paper-lined muffin cups. Bake at 350°F 21 to 24 minutes or until toothpick inserted into centers comes out clean.

Toll House® Mini Morsel Pancakes

2½ cups all-purpose flour
1 cup (6 ounces) NESTLÉ® TOLL HOUSE® Semi-Sweet Chocolate
    Mini Morsels
1 tablespoon baking powder
½ teaspoon salt
1¾ cups milk
2 large eggs
⅓ cup vegetable oil
⅓ cup packed brown sugar
    Powdered sugar
    Fresh sliced strawberries (optional)
    Maple syrup

COMBINE flour, morsels, baking powder and salt in large bowl. Combine milk, eggs, vegetable oil and brown sugar in medium bowl; add to flour mixture. Stir just until moistened. (Batter may be lumpy.)

HEAT griddle or skillet over medium heat; brush lightly with vegetable oil. Pour ¼ cup of batter onto hot griddle; cook until bubbles begin to burst. Turn; continue to cook for about 1 minute longer or until golden. Repeat with *remaining* batter.

SPRINKLE with powdered sugar; top with strawberries. Serve with maple syrup. *Makes about 18 pancakes*

Cheeseburger Chowder

1 pound ground beef
1 large onion, chopped (about 1 cup)
2 cans (26 ounces each) CAMPBELL'S® Condensed Cream of
    Mushroom Soup (Regular or 98% Fat Free)
2 soup cans milk
1 cup finely shredded Cheddar cheese (about 4 ounces)
1 cup PEPPERIDGE FARM® Seasoned Croutons

1. Cook the beef and onion in a 3-quart saucepan over medium-high heat until the beef is well browned, stirring often to separate the meat. Pour off any fat.

2. Stir the soup and milk in the saucepan. Cook until the mixture is hot and bubbling. Stir in ½ **cup** cheese. Cook and stir until the cheese is melted.

3. Divide the soup among **8** serving bowls. Top **each** bowl with **1 tablespoon** remaining cheese and **2 tablespoons** croutons.

Makes 8 servings

Prep Time: 10 minutes • Cook Time: 20 minutes

Nancy's Chicken Noodle Soup

1 can (about 48 ounces) chicken broth
2 boneless skinless chicken breasts, cut into bite-size pieces
4 cups water
⅔ cup diced onion
⅔ cup diced celery
⅔ cup diced carrots
⅔ cup sliced mushrooms
½ cup frozen peas
4 chicken bouillon cubes
2 tablespoons butter
1 tablespoon dried parsley flakes
1 teaspoon salt
1 teaspoon ground cumin
1 teaspoon dried marjoram
1 teaspoon black pepper
2 cups cooked egg noodles

Slow Cooker Directions

Combine all ingredients except noodles in slow cooker. Cover; cook on LOW 5 to 7 hours or on HIGH 3 to 4 hours. Stir in noodles 30 minutes before serving.
Makes 4 servings

Ground herbs and spices tend to lose some flavor during the long cooking times in a slow cooker. It's best to taste and adjust seasonings just before serving. Adding some fresh herbs at the last minute will brighten flavors and add a fresh taste to slow-cooked soups.

Beef Stew with a Coffee Kick

⅓ cup all-purpose flour
1 teaspoon salt
½ teaspoon garlic powder
½ teaspoon dried marjoram
½ teaspoon black pepper
3 tablespoons vegetable oil
2 pounds beef stew meat, cut into 1½-inch cubes
1 can (about 14 ounces) diced tomatoes
1¼ cups strong brewed coffee, at room temperature
2 teaspoons beef bouillon granules
2 cups cubed potatoes
4 stalks celery, sliced
4 medium carrots, sliced
3 small onions, quartered
1 bay leaf

1. Preheat oven to 325°F. Whisk together flour, salt, garlic powder, marjoram and pepper in small bowl.

2. Heat oil in Dutch oven over medium-high heat. Brown meat on all sides in batches. Sprinkle flour mixture over meat. Cook and stir about 2 minutes or until flour is slightly browned. Stir in tomatoes, coffee and bouillon granules. Mix well, scraping up browned bits on bottom of Dutch oven. Bring to a simmer; stir in potatoes, celery, carrots, onions and bay leaf.

3. Cover; bake 2½ to 3 hours or until meat is tender, stirring every hour. Remove bay leaf before serving.   *Makes 6 servings*

Tip: For a thinner stew, add ½ to ¾ cup coffee 15 minutes before serving.

Bacon Potato Chowder

4 slices bacon
1 large onion, chopped (about 1 cup)
4 cans (10¾ ounces each) CAMPBELL'S® Condensed Cream of
    Potato Soup
4 soup cans milk
¼ teaspoon ground black pepper
2 large russet potatoes, cut into ½-inch pieces (about 3 cups)
2 cups shredded Cheddar cheese (8 ounces)
½ cup chopped fresh chives

1. Cook bacon in 6-quart saucepot over medium-high heat until it's crisp. Remove bacon with a fork and drain on paper towels. Crumble the bacon.

2. Add the onion and cook in the hot drippings until tender.

3. Stir the soup, milk, black pepper and potatoes into the saucepot. Heat to a boil. Reduce the heat to low. Cover and cook for 15 minutes or until the potatoes are tender. Remove from the heat.

4. Add the cheese and stir until the cheese melts. Serve with the chives.

Makes 8 servings

Transporting Tip: Transfer the chowder to a slow cooker. Chowder tends to thicken upon standing, so bring along some SWANSON® Vegetable or Chicken Broth to stir in before serving.

Prep Time: 15 minutes • Cook Time: 30 minutes

Tomato Soup

1 tablespoon vegetable oil
1 cup chopped onion
2 cloves garlic, minced
½ cup chopped carrot
¼ cup chopped celery
2 cans (28 ounces each) crushed tomatoes in tomato purée
3½ cups chicken broth
1 tablespoon Worcestershire sauce
½ teaspoon salt
½ teaspoon dried thyme
¼ to ½ teaspoon black pepper
2 to 4 drops hot pepper sauce

1. Heat oil in large saucepan or Dutch oven over medium-high heat. Add onion and garlic; cook and stir 2 minutes or until onion is soft. Add carrot and celery; cook and stir 7 to 9 minutes or until tender.

2. Stir in tomatoes, broth, Worcestershire sauce, salt, thyme, black pepper and hot pepper sauce. Reduce heat to low. Cover and simmer 20 minutes, stirring frequently.

3. For smoother soup, remove from heat. Let cool about 10 minutes. Process soup in small batches in food processor or blender until smooth. Return soup to saucepan; simmer 3 to 5 minutes or until heated through.

Makes 6 servings

Chili in Tortilla Bowls

1½ pounds ground turkey or ground beef
1 medium onion, chopped
1 large red bell pepper, diced
2 tablespoons chili powder
1 can (19 ounces) red kidney beans, rinsed and drained
1 can (11 ounces) whole kernel corn, drained
1 jar (1 pound 10 ounces) RAGÚ® Chunky Pasta Sauce
6 burrito-size whole wheat, spinach or tomato tortillas
1 cup shredded 2% Cheddar cheese (about 4 ounces)

1. In 12-inch skillet, brown ground turkey over medium-high heat, stirring occasionally. Add onion, red pepper and chili powder and cook, stirring occasionally, 5 minutes or until onion is tender. Stir in beans, corn and Pasta Sauce.

2. Bring to a boil over high heat. Reduce heat to low and simmer, covered, stirring occasionally, 20 minutes.

3. Meanwhile, using one tortilla at a time, press into a 1- or 2-cup microwave-safe bowl to form bowl shape. Microwave at HIGH 1½ minutes. Let cool 1 minute. Gently lift out and arrange on serving plate. Repeat with remaining tortillas.

4. To serve, spoon chili into tortilla bowls, then sprinkle with cheese.

Makes 6 servings

Prep Time: 10 minutes • Cook Time: 25 minutes

New England Clam Chowder

Nonstick cooking spray
4 ounces smoked turkey sausage, finely chopped
1½ cups chopped onions
2¾ cups milk
2 medium red potatoes, diced
2 cans (6½ ounces each) minced clams, drained, liquid reserved
2 bay leaves
½ teaspoon dried thyme
2 tablespoons butter
¼ teaspoon black pepper

1. Spray Dutch oven with cooking spray; heat over medium-high heat. Cook and stir sausage 2 minutes or until browned. Transfer to plate.

2. Add onions; cook and stir 2 minutes. Add milk, potatoes, reserved clam liquid, bay leaves and thyme. Simmer, covered, 15 minutes or until potatoes are tender.

3. Remove bay leaves. Stir in sausage, clams, butter and pepper. Simmer 5 minutes or until heated through.   *Makes 4 servings*

For richer chowder, use only 2 cups of milk. Add ¾ of a cup of half and half or whipping cream in step 3. Garnish bowls of chowder with snipped fresh chives. Serve the chowder with saltines or oyster crackers and pass hot pepper sauce for those who want to spice things up a bit.

Vegetable Minestrone Soup

2 tablespoons olive or vegetable oil
2 medium zucchini, cut in half lengthwise and thickly sliced (about
    3 cups)
2 cloves garlic, minced
½ teaspoon dried rosemary leaves, crushed
4 cups SWANSON® Vegetable Broth (Regular or Certified Organic)
1 can (about 14½ ounces) diced tomatoes, drained
1 can (about 19 ounces) white kidney beans (cannellini), rinsed and
    drained
½ cup uncooked corkscrew-shaped pasta (rotini)
¼ cup grated Parmesan cheese (optional)

1. Heat the oil in a 6-quart saucepot. Add the zucchini, garlic and rosemary and cook until the zucchini is tender-crisp.

2. Stir the broth and tomatoes in the saucepot and heat to a boil. Reduce the heat to low. Cover and cook for 10 minutes.

3. Increase the heat to medium. Stir in the beans and pasta. Cook for 10 minutes or until the pasta is tender. Serve with the cheese, if desired.

Makes 8 servings

Prep Time: 10 minutes • **Cook Time:** 30 minutes

Beer-Braised Chili

2 tablespoons vegetable oil
2 pounds boneless beef chuck roast or stew meat, cut into ¾-inch
    cubes
1 large onion, chopped
4 cloves garlic, minced
1 tablespoon chili powder
1 tablespoon ground cumin
1¼ teaspoons salt
1 teaspoon dried oregano
½ teaspoon ground red pepper
1 can (about 14 ounces) Mexican-style stewed tomatoes, undrained
1 bottle or can (12 ounces) beer (not dark)
½ cup salsa
1 can (about 15 ounces) black beans, rinsed and drained
1 can (about 15 ounces) red beans or pinto beans, rinsed and
    drained

Optional Toppings
    Chopped cilantro, thinly sliced green onions, shredded Chihuahua
    or Cheddar cheese, sliced pickled jalapeño peppers, sour cream

1. Heat oil in large saucepan or Dutch oven over medium-high heat.
Add beef, onion and garlic; cook and stir 5 minutes. Sprinkle chili
powder, cumin, salt, oregano and red pepper over mixture; mix well.
Add tomatoes, beer and salsa; bring to a boil. Reduce heat; cover and
simmer 1¼ hours or until beef is very tender, stirring once.

2. Stir in beans. Simmer, uncovered, 20 minutes or until slightly
thickened. Serve with desired toppings.   *Makes 6 servings*

Hearty Beef Barley Stew

2 cups baby carrots
1 package (10 ounces) fresh mushrooms, sliced
1½ pounds boneless beef chuck steak, cut into 1-inch cubes
1 envelope LIPTON® RECIPE SECRETS® Onion Soup Mix
2 cans (14½ ounces each) beef broth
1 can (14½ ounces) diced tomatoes, undrained
2 cups water
¾ cup uncooked pearl barley
1 cup frozen green peas
Salt and ground black pepper, to taste

Slow Cooker Directions

1. In slow cooker, layer carrots, mushrooms and beef. Combine LIPTON® RECIPE SECRETS® Onion Soup Mix, broth, tomatoes, water and barley; pour over beef.

2. Cook, covered, on low 8 to 10 hours or on high 4 to 6 hours, or until beef is tender.

3. Stir in peas and cook, covered, 5 minutes, or until heated through. Season, if desired, with salt and ground black pepper.

Makes 8 servings

Prep Time: 10 minutes • **Cook Time:** High 4 hours, 5 minutes

Beefy Broccoli & Cheese Soup

2 cups chicken broth
1 package (10 ounces) frozen chopped broccoli
¼ cup chopped onion
¼ pound ground beef
1 cup milk
2 tablespoons all-purpose flour
1 cup (4 ounces) shredded sharp Cheddar cheese
1½ teaspoons chopped fresh oregano *or* ½ teaspoon dried oregano
Salt and black pepper
Hot pepper sauce

1. Bring broth to a boil in medium saucepan. Add broccoli and onion; cook 5 minutes or until broccoli is tender.

2. Meanwhile, brown ground beef 6 to 8 minutes in small skillet over medium-high heat, stirring to break up meat. Drain fat. Gradually add milk to flour in small bowl, mixing until well blended. Add milk mixture and ground beef to broth mixture; cook, stirring constantly, until mixture is thickened and bubbly.

3. Add cheese and oregano; stir until cheese is melted. Season to taste with salt, black pepper and hot pepper sauce.   *Makes 4 servings*

BURGERS & MORE

Stuffed Fiesta Burgers

1 pound ground beef
1 package (1¼ ounces) TACO BELL® HOME ORIGINALS® Taco
  Seasoning Mix
¼ cup PHILADELPHIA® Chive & Onion Cream Cheese Spread
⅓ cup KRAFT® Shredded Cheddar Cheese
4 hamburger buns, split, lightly toasted
½ cup TACO BELL® HOME ORIGINALS® Thick 'N Chunky Medium
  Salsa
1 avocado, peeled, pitted and cut into 8 slices

1. Preheat grill to medium heat. Mix meat and seasoning mix. Shape
into 8 thin patties. Mix cream cheese spread and shredded cheese.
Spoon about 2 tablespoons of the cheese mixture onto center of each
of 4 of the patties; top with second patty. Pinch edges of patties together
to seal.

2. Grill 7 to 9 minutes on each side or until cooked through (160°F).

3. Cover bottom halves of buns with burgers. Top with salsa, avocados
and top halves of buns.   *Makes 4 servings*

Prep Time: 15 minutes • Grill Time: 9 minutes

Grilled Reubens with Coleslaw

    2 cups sauerkraut
    ¼ cup (½ stick) butter, softened
    8 slices rye or marble rye bread
  12 ounces thinly-sliced deli corned beef or pastrami
    4 slices Swiss cheese
    ¼ to ½ cup prepared Thousand Island dressing
    2 cups deli coleslaw
    4 pickle spears

1. Preheat indoor grill or large grill pan. Drain sauerkraut well in colander.

2. Spread butter evenly over 1 side of each slice of bread. Turn 4 bread slices over; top with equal amounts corned beef, sauerkraut and cheese. Top with remaining 4 bread slices, butter side up.

3. Grill sandwiches 4 minutes or just until cheese begins to melt.

4. Spread dressing over corned beef just before serving. Serve with coleslaw and pickles.   *Makes 4 servings*

Note: Stack sandwich ingredients in the order given to prevent sogginess.

Philadelphia Cheesesteaks

2 tablespoons vegetable oil
1 large onion, sliced (about 1 cup)
1 large red or green pepper, thinly sliced (about 1½ cups)
1 cup sliced mushrooms
4 frozen sandwich steaks (about 2 ounces each)
1 can (10¾ ounces) CAMPBELL'S® Condensed Cheddar Cheese Soup
4 (8-inch) long hard rolls, split

1. Heat the oil in a 12-inch skillet over medium-high heat. Add the onion, pepper and mushrooms and cook until the vegetables are tender. Remove the vegetables from the skillet.

2. Add the steaks to the skillet. Cook and stir until they're cooked through.

3. Spoon the soup into a microwavable bowl. Cover and microwave on HIGH for 1½ minutes or until it's hot. Stir.

4. Spread **each** roll with **2 tablespoons** soup. Divide the steaks and vegetables among the rolls and top with the remaining soup.

Makes 4 sandwiches

Kitchen Tip: Try using prepared garlic bread instead of the rolls in this recipe.

Prep Time: 10 minutes • Cook Time: 10 minutes

Portobello Mushroom Burgers

2 teaspoons olive oil, divided
¾ cup thinly sliced shallots
4 large portobello mushrooms, stems removed
   Salt and black pepper
2 cloves garlic, minced
¼ cup mayonnaise
2 tablespoons chopped fresh basil
4 whole-grain hamburger buns
4 ounces fresh mozzarella cheese, sliced
2 roasted red bell peppers, cut into strips

1. Heat 1 teaspoon oil in medium saucepan over medium heat. Add shallots; cook and stir 6 to 8 minutes or until golden brown and soft. Set aside.

2. Preheat broiler.

3. Drizzle each mushroom on both sides with remaining 1 teaspoon oil; season both sides with salt and black pepper. Place mushrooms, cap side down, on foil-lined baking sheet. Sprinkle with garlic. Broil mushrooms 4 minutes per side.

4. Combine mayonnaise and basil in small bowl. Spread buns with basil mayonnaise. Fill buns with mozzarella slices, shallots, mushrooms and bell pepper strips.   *Makes 4 burgers*

Easy Patty Melts

3 to 4 tablespoons butter, divided
1 large onion, thinly sliced
8 slices rye bread
8 slices Cheddar or mozzarella cheese
   Spicy Barbecued Meat Loaf (recipe on page 76), cut into 4 slices
   Ketchup (optional)

1. Heat 1 tablespoon butter in large skillet over medium-high heat. Add onion; cover and cook 5 minutes or until onion is transparent. Uncover; cook and stir 8 to 10 minutes or until golden brown and very tender.

2. Top each of 4 slices of bread with a slice of cheese, a slice of meatloaf, onion, another slice of cheese and remaining bread.

3. Melt 1½ tablespoons butter in large skillet over medium heat. Add 2 sandwiches; cook, turning occasionally, 10 to 12 minutes or until golden brown and cheese is melted. Repeat with remaining butter and sandwiches. Serve with ketchup, if desired.   *Makes 4 servings*

If you don't have leftover meat loaf to make these patty melts, leftover burgers will work almost as well. It's important to cook the onion long enough so that it caramelizes and becomes thoroughly browned without burning. This process brings out the onion's sweetness.

Deluxe Bacon & Gouda Burgers

1½ pounds ground beef
   Salt and black pepper
⅓ cup mayonnaise
1 teaspoon minced garlic
¼ teaspoon Dijon mustard
2 thick slices red onion
4 to 8 slices Gouda cheese
4 onion rolls, split and toasted
   Butter lettuce leaves
   Tomato slices
4 to 8 slices bacon, crisp-cooked

1. Prepare grill for direct cooking. Shape beef into 4 patties about ¾ inch thick. Season burgers with salt and pepper. Cover and refrigerate. Combine mayonnaise, garlic and mustard in small bowl; mix well. Set aside.

2. Place patties and onion on grid over medium-high heat. Grill, covered, 8 to 10 minutes (or uncovered, 13 to 15 minutes) or until cooked through (160°F), turning occasionally. Remove onion when slightly browned. Top burgers with cheese during last 2 minutes of grilling.

3. Arrange lettuce on bottom half of each roll; top with mayonnaise mixture, burger, tomato, onion and bacon.   *Makes 4 burgers*

Substitution: Use a prepared mayonnaise spread instead of the garlic mayonnaise in this recipe.

Apple Monte Cristos

4 ounces Gouda cheese, shredded
1 ounce cream cheese, softened
2 teaspoons honey
½ teaspoon ground cinnamon
4 slices cinnamon raisin bread
1 small apple, cored and thinly sliced
¼ cup milk
1 egg, beaten
1 tablespoon butter
   Powdered sugar

1. Combine Gouda cheese, cream cheese, honey and cinnamon in small bowl; stir until well blended. Spread cheese mixture evenly on all bread slices. Layer apple slices evenly over cheese on 2 bread slices; top with remaining bread slices.

2. Combine milk and egg in shallow bowl; stir until well blended. Dip sandwiches in egg mixture, turning to coat well.

3. Melt butter in large nonstick skillet over medium heat. Add sandwiches; cook 4 to 5 minutes per side or until cheese melts and sandwiches are golden brown. Sprinkle with powdered sugar.

Makes 2 sandwiches

Chicken Burgers with White Cheddar

1¼ pounds ground chicken
1 cup plain dry bread crumbs
½ cup diced red bell pepper
½ cup ground walnuts
¼ cup sliced green onions
¼ cup light-colored beer
2 tablespoons chopped fresh parsley
2 tablespoons lemon juice
2 cloves garlic, minced
¾ teaspoon salt
⅛ teaspoon black pepper
    Nonstick cooking spray
4 slices white Cheddar cheese
4 whole wheat buns
    Dijon mustard
    Lettuce leaves

1. Combine chicken, bread crumbs, bell pepper, walnuts, green onions, beer, parsley, lemon juice, garlic, salt and black pepper in large bowl; mix lightly. Shape into 4 patties.

2. Spray large skillet with cooking spray; heat over medium-high heat. Cook patties 6 to 7 minutes on each side or until cooked through (165°F). Place cheese on patties; cover skillet just until cheese melts.

3. Serve burgers on buns with mustard and lettuce.

Makes 4 servings

Grilled Veggie Sandwiches

2 tablespoons WISH-BONE® Light Italian Dressing
1 small portobello mushroom
1 small red bell pepper, quartered
3 ounces fresh mozzarella cheese, thinly sliced
4 fresh basil leaves
4 thick slices Italian bread
2 tablespoons HELLMANN'S® or BEST FOODS® Light Mayonnaise

Brush WISH-BONE® Light Italian Dressing on mushroom and bell pepper. Grill, turning once, 8 minutes or until tender; slice.

Arrange mushroom, bell pepper, cheese and basil on 2 bread slices, then top with remaining 2 bread slices. Spread HELLMANN'S® or BEST FOODS® Light Mayonnaise on outside of sandwiches.

Cook sandwiches in 12-inch nonstick skillet or grill over medium heat, turning once, 6 minutes or until bread is toasted and cheese is melted.

Makes 2 servings

Tip: Try this sandwich spread for a change of pace: Combine sun-dried tomatoes and chopped fresh basil with HELLMANN'S® or BEST FOODS® Light Mayonnaise.

Prep Time: 15 minutes • Cook Time: 15 minutes

Grilled Wisconsin Triple Cheese Sandwich

12 slices whole grain bread
¼ cup whole grain Dijon style mustard
6 slices (1 ounce each) baked ham
6 slices (¾ ounce each) Wisconsin Provolone cheese
6 slices (¾ ounce each) Wisconsin Cheddar cheese
1 cup (6 ounces) crumbled Wisconsin Gorgonzola cheese

Prepare grill; heat until coals are ash white. Meanwhile, spread each slice of bread with mustard. Top each of 6 slices of bread with 1 slice ham, 1 slice Provolone and 1 slice Cheddar. Sprinkle with Gorgonzola cheese. Top each sandwich with remaining bread. Grill over hot coals, turning once, until cheese is melted, about 3 minutes per side.

Makes 6 sandwiches

Favorite recipe from **Wisconsin Milk Marketing Board**

Bacon Burgers

8 slices bacon, crisp-cooked
4 pounds ground beef
1½ teaspoons chopped fresh thyme *or* ½ teaspoon dried thyme
½ teaspoon salt
Dash black pepper
4 slices Swiss cheese

1. Prepare grill for direct cooking. Crumble 4 slices bacon.

2. Combine ground beef, crumbled bacon, thyme, salt and pepper in medium bowl; mix lightly. Shape into 4 patties.

3. Place patties on grid over medium heat. Grill, covered, 8 to 10 minutes (or uncovered, 13 to 15 minutes) or until cooked through (160°F), turning halfway through grilling. Top with cheese during last 2 minutes of grilling. Serve with remaining bacon slices.

Makes 4 burgers

Pulled Pork Sandwiches

2 tablespoons kosher salt
2 tablespoons packed light brown sugar
2 tablespoons paprika
1 teaspoon dry mustard
1 teaspoon black pepper
1 boneless pork shoulder roast (about 3 pounds)
1½ cups stout
½ cup cider vinegar
6 to 8 large hamburger buns, split
¾ cup barbecue sauce

1. Preheat oven to 325°F. Combine salt, sugar, paprika, dry mustard and pepper in small bowl; mix well. Rub into pork.

2. Place pork in 4-quart Dutch oven. Add stout and vinegar. Cover; bake 3 hours or until meat is fork-tender. Cool 15 to 30 minutes or until cool enough to handle.

3. Shred pork into pieces using fork. Serve on buns with barbecue sauce.   *Makes 6 to 8 servings*

Tip: This recipe is a great dish for a summer or fall picnic or party. Baked beans, corn on the cob and watermelon are wonderful accompaniments.

Mediterranean Burgers

1 ½ pounds ground beef
2 tablespoons grated Parmesan cheese
2 tablespoons chopped kalamata olives
1 tablespoon chopped fresh parsley
1 tablespoon diced tomato
2 teaspoons dried oregano
1 teaspoon black pepper
4 slices mozzarella cheese
4 hamburger buns, split
Lettuce leaves
Roasted red pepper strips

1. Prepare grill for direct cooking.

2. Combine beef, Parmesan cheese, olives, parsley, tomato, oregano and pepper in medium bowl; mix lightly. Shape into four ½-inch-thick patties.

3. Grill patties over medium heat, covered, 8 to 10 minutes (or uncovered, 13 to 15 minutes) or until cooked through (160°F), turning halfway through grilling. Top with cheese during last 2 minutes of grilling. Fill buns with lettuce, burgers and roasted red pepper.

Makes 4 burgers

Salisbury Steaks with Mushroom-Wine Sauce

  1 pound ground beef
  ¾ teaspoon garlic salt or seasoned salt
  ¼ teaspoon black pepper
  2 tablespoons butter
  1 package (8 ounces) sliced mushrooms
  2 tablespoons sweet vermouth or ruby port wine
  1 jar (12 ounces) *or* 1 can (10½ ounces) beef gravy

1. Combine beef, garlic salt and pepper in medium bowl; mix gently. Shape into 4 oval patties.

2. Heat large nonstick skillet over medium-high heat. Place patties in skillet; cook 3 minutes per side or until browned. Transfer to plate. Pour off drippings.

3. Melt butter in same skillet; add mushrooms. Cook and stir 2 minutes. Add vermouth; cook 1 minute. Add gravy; mix well.

4. Return patties to skillet. Simmer, uncovered, over medium heat, stirring occasionally, 2 minutes or until cooked through (160°F).

Makes 4 servings

Prep and Cook Time: 20 minutes

Creamy Bow-Tie Pasta with Chicken and Broccoli

3 cups (8 ounces) farfalle (bow-tie pasta), uncooked
4 cups broccoli florets
3 tablespoons KRAFT® Roasted Red Pepper Italian with Parmesan
    Dressing
6 small boneless, skinless chicken breast halves (1½ pounds)
2 cloves garlic, minced
2 cups tomato-basil spaghetti sauce
4 ounces (½ of 8-ounce package) PHILADELPHIA® Neufchâtel
    Cheese, ⅓ Less Fat than Cream Cheese, cubed
¼ cup KRAFT® 100% Grated Parmesan Cheese

1. Cook pasta as directed on package, adding broccoli to the cooking water for the last 3 minutes of the pasta cooking time. Meanwhile, heat dressing in large nonstick skillet on medium heat. Add chicken and garlic; cook 5 minutes. Turn chicken over; continue cooking 4 to 5 minutes or until chicken is cooked through (170°F).

2. Drain pasta mixture in colander; return to pan and set aside. Add spaghetti sauce and Neufchâtel cheese to chicken in skillet; cook on medium-low heat 2 to 3 minutes or until Neufchâtel cheese is completely melted, mixture is well blended and chicken is coated with sauce, stirring occasionally. Remove chicken from skillet; keep warm. Add sauce mixture to pasta mixture; mix well. Transfer to six serving bowls.

3. Cut chicken crosswise into thick slices; fan out chicken over pasta mixture. Sprinkle evenly with Parmesan cheese.

Makes 6 servings, about 1½ cups each

Substitute: Prepare as directed, using whole wheat or multigrain pasta.

Prep Time: 10 minutes • Cook Time: 15 minutes

Spicy Barbecued Meat Loaf

1 to 2 slices rye bread, torn into pieces
1 large onion, cut into chunks
3 cloves garlic, peeled
1 tablespoon butter
1 pound ground beef
1 pound bulk pork sausage
2 eggs
¾ cup hickory-flavored barbecue sauce, divided
¾ teaspoon salt
¼ teaspoon pepper

1. Preheat oven to 375°F. Line jelly-roll pan or shallow roasting pan with foil.

2. Process torn bread in food processor to make crumbs. Transfer ¾ cup bread crumbs to large bowl; set aside. (Any remaining crumbs may be frozen up to 3 months.) Add onion and garlic to food processor; process until finely chopped.

3. Melt butter in large skillet over medium heat. Add onion mixture; cook and stir 6 minutes or until softened. Let cool 5 minutes.

4. Add beef, sausage, eggs, ¼ cup barbecue sauce, salt and pepper to reserved bread crumbs. Add onion mixture; mix well.

5. Transfer meat mixture to prepared pan; form into 9×6-inch oval. Bake 30 minutes. Spread remaining ½ cup barbecue sauce over meat loaf. Bake 30 minutes more or until cooked through (160°F). Let stand 5 minutes before slicing. Reserve half of meat loaf for Easy Patty Melts (page 56), if desired. *Makes 8 servings*

Garlicky Oven-Fried Chicken Thighs

1 egg
2 tablespoons water
1 cup plain dry bread crumbs
1 teaspoon salt
1 teaspoon garlic powder
½ teaspoon black pepper
¼ teaspoon ground red pepper
8 chicken thighs (about 3 pounds)
   Olive oil cooking spray

1. Preheat oven to 350°F.

2. Beat egg slightly with water in shallow bowl; set aside. Mix bread crumbs with salt, garlic powder, black pepper and red pepper in separate shallow bowl.

3. Dip chicken thighs into egg mixture; turn to coat. Transfer to bread crumb mixture; press lightly to coat both sides. Place, skin side up, on large baking sheet.

4. Lightly spray chicken with cooking spray. Bake 50 to 60 minutes or until browned and cooked through (165°F). *Do not turn chicken during cooking.*   *Makes 4 servings*

Variations: Substitute flavored bread crumbs for the plain bread crumbs, salt, garlic powder, black pepper and red pepper. Or substitute your favorite dried herbs or spices for the garlic powder and red pepper. Thyme, sage, oregano or rosemary would be delicious, as would Cajun or Creole seasoning.

Cobb Salad

1 package (10 ounces) torn mixed salad greens *or* 8 cups torn
    romaine lettuce
6 ounces cooked chicken breast, cut into bite-size pieces
1 tomato, seeded and chopped
2 hard-cooked eggs, cut into bite-size pieces
4 slices bacon, crisp-cooked and crumbled
1 ripe avocado, diced
1 large carrot, shredded
2 ounces blue cheese, crumbled
    Blue cheese or other dressing

Place lettuce in serving bowl. Arrange chicken, tomato, eggs, bacon,
avocado, carrot and cheese on top of lettuce. Serve with dressing.

Makes 4 servings

Turkey Club Salad

8 cups coarsely chopped romaine lettuce leaves
2 large hard-cooked eggs, diced
1 cup cherry tomatoes, halved
4 slices bacon, crisp-cooked and crumbled
1 package (4 ounces) blue cheese crumbles
8 slices deli turkey breast, rolled-up
½ cup WISH-BONE® Ranch Dressing

Arrange lettuce on large platter. Top with rows of eggs, tomatoes, bacon,
cheese and turkey. Just before serving, drizzle with WISH-BONE® Ranch
Dressing.

Makes 4 servings

Prep Time: 15 minutes

Fish & Chips

¾ cup all-purpose flour
½ cup flat beer or lemon-lime carbonated beverage
    Vegetable oil
 4 medium russet potatoes, each cut into 8 wedges
    Salt
 1 egg, separated
 1 pound cod fillets (about 6 to 8 small fillets)
    Malt vinegar and lemon wedges (optional)

1. Combine flour, beer and 2 teaspoons oil in small bowl. Cover; refrigerate 1 to 2 hours.

2. Pour 2 inches oil into large heavy saucepan. Heat over medium heat to 365°F. Add potato wedges in batches. (Do not crowd.) Fry potato wedges 4 to 6 minutes or until browned, turning once. (Allow temperature of oil to return to 365°F between batches.) Drain on paper towels; sprinkle lightly with salt. Reserve oil to fry cod.

3. Stir egg yolk into reserved flour mixture. Beat egg white in medium bowl with electric mixer at medium-high speed until soft peaks form. Fold egg white into flour mixture.

4. Return oil to 365°F. Dip fish pieces into batter in batches; fry 4 to 6 minutes or until batter is crispy and brown and fish begins to flake when tested with fork, turning once. (Allow temperature of oil to return to 365°F between batches.) Drain on paper towels. Serve immediately with potato wedges. Sprinkle with vinegar and serve with lemon wedges, if desired. *Makes 4 servings*

Roasted Chicken & Vegetables

1 REYNOLDS® Oven Bag, Large Size
1 tablespoon flour
2 cloves garlic, minced
2 tablespoons *each* olive oil and fresh lemon juice
2 teaspoons dried Italian seasoning
1 whole chicken (3½ to 4 pounds)
2 cups peeled baby carrots, halved lengthwise
1 medium red bell pepper, cut in cubes
1 medium onion, cut in small wedges
  Seasoned salt and black pepper to taste

PREHEAT oven to 350°F.

SHAKE flour in Reynolds Oven Bag; place in 13×9×2-inch or larger baking pan.

ADD garlic, olive oil, lemon juice and Italian seasoning to oven bag. Turn bag to mix with flour. Place chicken in bag. Turn bag to coat chicken with olive oil mixture. Arrange vegetables around chicken. Sprinkle seasoned salt and pepper over chicken and vegetables.

CLOSE oven bag with nylon tie; cut six ½-inch slits in top. Tuck ends of bag in pan.

BAKE 50 to 60 minutes or until meat thermometer reads 180°F.

Makes 4 to 6 servings

Prep Time: 20 minutes • Cook Time: 50 minutes

Garlic Mashed Potatoes & Beef Bake

1 pound ground beef
1 can (10¾ ounces) CAMPBELL'S® Condensed Cream of Mushroom
 with Roasted Garlic Soup
1 tablespoon Worcestershire sauce
1 bag (16 ounces) frozen vegetable combination (broccoli,
 cauliflower, carrots), thawed
2 cups water
3 tablespoons butter
¾ cup milk
2 cups instant mashed potato flakes

1. Heat the oven to 400°F. Cook the beef in a 10-inch skillet over medium-high heat until it's well browned, stirring often to separate meat. Pour off any fat.

2. Stir the beef, ½ **can** soup, Worcestershire and vegetables in a 2-quart shallow baking dish.

3. Heat the water, butter and remaining soup in a 3-quart saucepan over medium heat to a boil. Remove the saucepan from the heat. Stir in the milk. Stir in the potatoes. Spoon the potatoes over the beef mixture.

4. Bake for 20 minutes or until the potatoes are lightly browned.

Makes 4 servings

Kitchen Tip: You can use your favorite frozen vegetable combination in this recipe.

Prep Time: 15 minutes • Bake Time: 20 minutes

Macaroni & Cheese with Bacon

3 cups (8 ounces) uncooked rotini pasta
2 tablespoons butter
2 tablespoons all-purpose flour
¼ teaspoon salt
¼ teaspoon dry mustard
⅛ teaspoon black pepper
1½ cups milk
2 cups (8 ounces) shredded sharp Cheddar cheese
8 ounces bacon, crisp-cooked and crumbled*
2 medium tomatoes, sliced

*1 cup cubed cooked ham may be substituted for the bacon.

1. Preheat oven to 350°F. Lightly grease shallow 1½-quart casserole.

2. Cook pasta according to package directions; drain and return to saucepan.

3. Melt butter in medium saucepan over medium-low heat. Whisk in flour, salt, mustard and pepper; cook and stir 1 minute. Whisk in milk. Bring to a boil over medium heat, stirring frequently. Reduce heat and simmer 2 minutes or until thickened. Remove from heat. Add cheese; stir until melted.

4. Add cheese mixture and bacon to pasta; stir until well blended. Transfer to prepared casserole. Bake 20 minutes. Arrange tomato slices on casserole. Bake 5 to 8 minutes or until casserole is bubbly and tomatoes are hot. *Makes 4 servings*

Oven-Barbecued Chicken

2 tablespoons vegetable oil, divided
1 large onion, chopped
⅓ cup dark brown sugar
⅓ cup cider vinegar
1 can (28 ounces) tomato purée
2 teaspoons chili powder
1 teaspoon mustard powder
1¼ teaspoons salt, divided
1 teaspoon black pepper, divided
¼ teaspoon liquid smoke
5 pounds chicken pieces

1. Heat 1 tablespoon oil in medium saucepan over medium-high heat. Add onion; cook and stir 5 minutes or until softened. Stir in brown sugar and vinegar. Add tomato purée, chili powder, mustard powder, 1 teaspoon salt, ¾ teaspoon pepper and liquid smoke, stirring to blend. Bring to a boil. Reduce heat and simmer 45 minutes or until mixture thickens slightly, stirring occasionally.

2. Preheat oven to 450°F. Place chicken pieces on baking sheet or jelly-roll pan. Brush chicken with remaining 1 tablespoon oil and sprinkle with remaining ¼ teaspoon salt and ¼ teaspoon pepper.

3. Roast chicken 35 minutes or until almost cooked through (160°F). *Turn oven to broil.* Spread sauce over chicken. Broil 6 inches from heat 10 minutes or until cooked through (165°F).   *Makes 8 to 10 servings*

Tip: As the sauce thickens, keep the heat low to keep spattering to a minimum, for both safety and ease in cleaning up. Refrigerate any extra sauce for later use.

Baked Pork Chops with Garden Stuffing

1 can (10¾ ounces) CAMPBELL'S® Condensed Golden Mushroom
    Soup
¾ cup water
1 bag (16 ounces) frozen vegetable combination (broccoli,
    cauliflower, carrots)
1 tablespoon butter
4 cups PEPPERIDGE FARM® Herb Seasoned Stuffing
6 bone-in pork chops, ¾-inch thick

1. Heat the oven to 400°F.

2. Heat ⅓ **cup** soup, ½ **cup** water, vegetables and butter in a 3-quart saucepan over medium heat to a boil. Remove the saucepan from the heat. Add the stuffing and mix lightly. Spoon the stuffing mixture into a greased 3-quart baking dish. Arrange the pork on the stuffing.

3. Stir the remaining soup and remaining water in a small bowl. Spoon the soup mixture over the pork.

4. Bake for 40 minutes or until the pork is cooked through.

Makes 6 servings

Kitchen Tip: You can try varying the vegetable combination or the stuffing flavor for a different spin on this recipe.

Prep Time: 15 minutes • Bake Time: 40 minutes

Oven Fries

2 small baking potatoes
2 teaspoons olive oil
¼ teaspoon salt or onion salt

1. Place potatoes in refrigerator 1 to 2 days.

2. Preheat oven to 450°F. Peel potatoes and cut lengthwise into ¼-inch-thick fries. Place in colander. Rinse under cold running water 2 minutes. Drain; pat dry with paper towels. Place potatoes in small resealable food storage bag. Drizzle with oil. Seal bag; shake to coat potatoes with oil.

3. Arrange potatoes in single layer on baking sheet. Bake 20 to 25 minutes or until light brown and crisp. Sprinkle with salt or onion salt.

Makes 2 servings

Note: Refrigerating potatoes—usually not recommended for storage—converts starch in the potatoes to sugar, which enhances the browning when the potatoes are baked. Do not refrigerate the potatoes longer than 2 days, because they might begin to taste too sweet.

Fresh Spinach-Strawberry Salad

¼ cup slivered almonds
1 bag (9 ounces) spinach leaves
¾ cup thinly sliced red onion
⅓ cup pomegranate juice
3 tablespoons sugar
3 tablespoons cider vinegar
2 tablespoons vegetable oil
2 tablespoons dark sesame oil
¼ teaspoon red pepper flakes
⅛ teaspoon salt
2 cups quartered strawberries
4 ounces crumbled goat cheese

1. Toast almonds in medium skillet over medium heat 2 minutes or until beginning to brown, stirring constantly. Remove to plate; set aside to cool.

2. Combine spinach and onion in large bowl.

3. Combine juice, sugar, vinegar, vegetable oil, sesame oil, pepper flakes and salt in jar with lid. Shake until well blended. Pour dressing over spinach and onion; toss gently to coat. Add strawberries; toss gently. Top with almonds and goat cheese.   *Makes 4 servings*

Variation: For a refreshing addition, add 1 to 2 teaspoons grated fresh ginger to the salad dressing.

Buttermilk Cornbread

REYNOLDS WRAP® Non-Stick Foil
2 cups buttermilk
2 eggs
¼ cup vegetable oil
2 cups yellow cornmeal
1 teaspoon baking soda
1 teaspoon baking powder
1 teaspoon salt

PREHEAT oven to 450°F. Line an 8-inch square baking pan with Reynolds Wrap Non-Stick Foil; set aside.

STIR together buttermilk, eggs and oil in a large bowl. Add cornmeal, baking soda, baking powder and salt; stir until well blended. Pour batter into foil-lined pan.

BAKE 25 to 30 minutes or until a wooden pick inserted in center comes out clean and cornbread is golden brown.   *Makes 9 servings*

Reynolds Kitchens Tip: To substitute regular milk for buttermilk, place 1 tablespoon lemon juice or vinegar in a measuring cup. Add enough milk to make 1 cup total liquid. Let stand 5 minutes before using.

Prep Time: 15 minutes • Cook Time: 25 minutes

Fried Green Tomatoes

  2 medium green tomatoes
  ¼ cup all-purpose flour
  ¼ cup yellow cornmeal
  ½ teaspoon salt
  ½ teaspoon garlic salt
  ½ teaspoon ground red pepper
  ½ teaspoon cracked black pepper
  1 cup buttermilk
  1 cup vegetable oil
    Hot pepper sauce (optional)

1. Cut tomatoes into ¼-inch-thick slices. Combine flour, cornmeal, salt, garlic salt, red pepper and black pepper in shallow bowl; mix well. Pour buttermilk into separate shallow bowl.

2. Heat oil in large skillet over medium heat. Dip tomato slices into buttermilk, coating both sides. Immediately dredge slices in flour mixture; shake off excess flour mixture.

3. Cook tomato slices in hot oil 3 to 5 minutes per side. Transfer to paper towels. Serve immediately with hot pepper sauce, if desired.

Makes 3 to 4 servings

Serving Suggestion: Serve fried green tomatoes on a bed of shredded lettuce as a first course.

Steamed Broccoli & Carrots

1 head broccoli (about 1 pound)
8 ounces baby carrots*
1 tablespoon butter
Salt and black pepper

*You may substitute ½ pound regular carrots cut into 2-inch chunks for the baby carrots.

1. Break broccoli into florets. Trim and discard large stems. Trim smaller stems; cut stems into thin slices.

2. Place 2 to 3 inches of water and steamer basket in large saucepan; bring to a boil.

3. Add broccoli and carrots; cover. Steam 6 minutes or until vegetables are crisp-tender.

4. Place vegetables in serving bowl. Add butter; toss lightly to coat. Season to taste with salt and pepper. *Makes 4 servings*

Garlic Mashed Potatoes

6 medium all-purpose potatoes, peeled, if desired, and cut into chunks (about 3 pounds)
Water
1 envelope LIPTON® RECIPE SECRETS® Savory Herb with Garlic Soup Mix*
½ cup milk
½ cup I CAN'T BELIEVE IT'S NOT BUTTER!® Spread

*Also terrific with LIPTON® RECIPE SECRETS® Onion or Golden Onion Soup Mix.

1. In 4-quart saucepan, cover potatoes with water; bring to a boil.

2. Reduce heat to low and simmer uncovered, 20 minutes or until potatoes are very tender; drain.

3. Return potatoes to saucepan, then mash. Stir in remaining ingredients. *Makes 8 servings*

Market Salad

3 eggs
4 cups mixed baby salad greens
2 cups green beans, cut into 1½-inch pieces, cooked and drained
4 thick slices bacon, crisp-cooked and crumbled
1 tablespoon minced fresh basil, chives or Italian parsley
3 tablespoons olive oil
1 tablespoon red wine vinegar
1 teaspoon Dijon mustard
¼ teaspoon salt
¼ teaspoon black pepper

1. Place eggs in small saucepan with water to cover; bring to a boil over medium-high heat. Immediately remove from heat. Cover; let stand 10 minutes. Drain; cool eggs to room temperature.

2. Combine salad greens, green beans, bacon and basil in large serving bowl. Peel and coarsely chop eggs; add to serving bowl. Whisk oil, vinegar, mustard, salt and pepper in small bowl until well blended; drizzle over salad. Toss gently to coat.   *Makes 4 servings*

To make mixing a salad dressing easier, place the ingredients in a jar that has a tight lid. Oil and vinegar won't stay mixed, so shake the jar right before pouring on the dressing. Better yet, pass the dressing jar and let everyone use as much as they want. Store leftovers right in the jar in the refrigerator. Allow the dressing to come to room temperature before remixing it.

Taco Chili Fries

1 bag (16 ounces) frozen French fries
2 pounds lean ground beef
1½ cups water
2 packets (1.25 ounces each) ORTEGA® Taco Seasoning Mix
1 cup ORTEGA® Salsa, any variety
1 can (15 ounces) JOAN OF ARC® black beans, drained
1 can (6 ounces) sliced black olives, drained
1 can (4 ounces) ORTEGA® Diced Green Chiles
2 cups (8 ounces) shredded Cheddar cheese
1 cup sour cream (optional)

Follow package directions for baking fries. Set aside.

Brown ground beef in medium skillet over medium-high heat. Stir in water and seasoning mix. Cook 5 minutes. Remove from heat.

Spoon salsa, beans, olives, chiles, cheese and sour cream, if desired, into separate bowls. Place fries in large bowl near meat mixture and toppings. Using heat-resistant ceramic plates, allow guests to create their own chili fries with meat and toppings. (Reserve sour cream until after mixture has been broiled.)

Place ceramic plate under broiler about 4 minutes or until fries reheat and cheese melts. Top with sour cream, if desired. Serve immediately.

Makes 6 servings

Note: Try using a variety of cheeses, from a jalapeño-Cheddar or Monterey Jack, to a stout blue cheese. Or offer a selection of diced fresh vegetables to top chili fries.

Prep Time: 15 minutes • Start to Finish: 45 minutes

Fruit Slaw

1 package (16 ounces) coleslaw mix
1 Granny Smith apple, cut into matchstick strips
1 D'Anjou pear, cut into matchstick strips
1 cup sliced strawberries
⅓ cup lemon juice
2 tablespoons mayonnaise
1 tablespoon sugar
2 teaspoons poppy seeds
1 teaspoon Dijon mustard
¼ teaspoon salt

1. Combine coleslaw mix, apple, pear and strawberries in large bowl.

2. Whisk lemon juice, mayonnaise, sugar, poppy seeds, mustard and salt in small bowl. Pour dressing over cabbage mixture; toss gently. Serve immediately. *Makes 6 to 8 servings*

Tip: To make ahead, prepare salad and dressing and store separately in refrigerator. Toss immediately before serving.

Carrot Raisin Salad

2 to 3 medium carrots, shredded* (1½ cups)
¼ cup raisins
¼ cup canned crushed pineapple, drained
1 tablespoon plain yogurt
4 lettuce leaves

*Packaged shredded carrots are available in the produce section, but this recipe is better with freshly shredded carrots.

1. Combine carrots, raisins, pineapple and yogurt in large bowl. Refrigerate 2 hours, stirring occasionally.

2. Serve on lettuce leaves. *Makes 4 servings*

Thick Potato Chips with Beer Ketchup

Beer Ketchup (recipe follows)
1 quart peanut oil
3 baking potatoes, scrubbed
Sea salt and black pepper

1. Prepare Beer Ketchup. Heat oil in large heavy saucepan (oil should come up sides at least 3 inches) to 345°F.

2. Slice potatoes into ¼-inch-thick slices. Lower into oil in batches. Fry 2 to 3 minutes per side, flipping to brown evenly on both sides. Drain on paper towels and immediately sprinkle with salt and pepper.

3. Serve with Beer Ketchup.   *Makes 4 servings*

Tip: If the potatoes begin browning too quickly, turn down the heat and wait for the oil to cool to the proper temperature. Too high a temperature will not cook the potatoes completely, and too low a temperature will make the chips soggy.

Beer Ketchup

¾ cup ketchup
¼ cup beer
1 tablespoon Worcestershire sauce
¼ teaspoon onion powder
Ground red pepper

Mix all ingredients in small saucepan. Bring to a boil. Reduce heat; simmer 2 to 3 minutes. Remove from heat and let cool. Cover and store in refrigerator until ready to use.   *Makes about 1 cup*

Best 'Cue Coleslaw

⅓ cup dill pickle relish
⅓ cup vegetable oil
3 tablespoons lime juice
2 tablespoons honey
1 teaspoon salt
1 teaspoon ground cumin
1 teaspoon ground red pepper
1 teaspoon black pepper
1 small head green cabbage, very thinly sliced
2 large carrots, shredded
1 bunch green onions, sliced
5 radishes, sliced

1. Combine relish, oil, lime juice, honey, salt, cumin, ground red pepper and black pepper in large bowl.

2. Add cabbage, carrots, green onions and radishes; stir until well combined. Chill at least 1 hour before serving.

Makes 6 to 8 servings

Tip: For a sweeter taste, add slivered apples instead of, or in addition to, the dill pickle relish.

Scalloped Tomatoes & Corn

1 can (15 ounces) cream-style corn
1 can (about 14 ounces) diced tomatoes, undrained
¾ cup saltine cracker crumbs
1 egg, lightly beaten
2 teaspoons sugar
¾ teaspoon black pepper
　Chopped fresh tomatoes (optional)
　Chopped fresh parsley (optional)

Slow Cooker Directions

1. Combine corn, tomatoes with juice, cracker crumbs, egg, sugar and pepper in slow cooker; mix well.

2. Cover; cook on LOW 4 to 6 hours or until set. Sprinkle with tomatoes and parsley before serving, if desired. *Makes 4 to 6 servings*

Prep Time: 7 minutes • Cook Time: 4 to 6 hours

Minestrone Salad

2 medium tomatoes, chopped
1 can (about 15 ounces) chickpeas, rinsed and drained
2 medium stalks celery, chopped
1 cup cooked macaroni
¼ cup shredded Parmesan cheese
2 tablespoons Italian dressing
　Salt and black pepper

Combine tomatoes, chickpeas, celery, macaroni, cheese and dressing in large bowl; toss well. Season with salt and pepper.

Makes 4 servings

Classic Apple Pie

1 package (15 ounces) refrigerated pie crusts
6 cups sliced Granny Smith, Crispin or other firm-fleshed apples
    (about 6 medium)
½ cup sugar
1 tablespoon cornstarch
2 teaspoons lemon juice
½ teaspoon ground cinnamon
½ teaspoon vanilla
⅛ teaspoon salt
⅛ teaspoon ground nutmeg
⅛ teaspoon ground cloves
1 tablespoon whipping cream

1. Preheat oven to 350°F. Line 9-inch pie pan with 1 pie crust. (Keep remaining pie crust in refrigerator until ready to use.)

2. Combine apples, sugar, cornstarch, lemon juice, cinnamon, vanilla, salt, nutmeg and cloves in large bowl; mix well. Pour into prepared crust. Place second crust over apples; crimp edge to seal.

3. Cut 4 slits in top crust; brush with cream. Bake 40 minutes or until crust is golden brown. Cool slightly before serving.

Makes 8 servings

Banana Pudding Cream Pie

1½ cups vanilla wafer crumbs (about 36 wafers)
⅓ cup butter or margarine, melted
¼ cup granulated sugar
1 (14-ounce) can EAGLE BRAND® Sweetened Condensed Milk (NOT evaporated milk)
4 egg yolks
1 (4-serving size) package cook-and-serve vanilla pudding and pie filling mix
½ cup water
1 (8-ounce) container sour cream, at room temperature
2 medium bananas, sliced, dipped in lemon juice and drained
Whipped cream
Additional banana slices, dipped in lemon juice and drained
Additional vanilla wafers

1. Preheat oven to 375°F. Combine wafer crumbs, butter and sugar; press firmly on bottom and up side to rim of 9-inch pie plate to form crust. Bake 8 to 10 minutes. Cool.

2. In heavy saucepan, combine EAGLE BRAND®, egg yolks, pudding mix and water; stir until well blended. Over medium heat, cook and stir until thickened and bubbly. Cool 15 minutes. Beat in sour cream.

3. Arrange banana slices on bottom of baked crust. Pour filling over bananas; cover. Chill. Top with whipped cream. Garnish with additional banana slices and vanilla wafers. Store leftovers covered in refrigerator.

Makes 1 (9-inch) pie

Prep Time: 20 minutes • Bake Time: 8 to 10 minutes

Chocolate Fruit Tarts

1 refrigerated pie crust (half of 15-ounce package)
1 ¼ cups prepared chocolate pudding (about 4 snack-size
      pudding cups)
Fresh berries

1. Let pie crust stand at room temperature 15 minutes. Spray back of standard (2½-inch) muffin pan with nonstick cooking spray.

2. Preheat oven to 450°F. Unroll crust onto clean work surface; cut out 6 circles with 4-inch round cookie cutter. Place crust circles over backs of alternate muffin cups, pinching crust into 5 or 6 pleats around sides of cups. (Press firmly to hold crust in place.) Prick bottom and sides with fork.

3. Bake about 8 minutes or until golden brown. Carefully remove tart shells from backs of muffin cups; cool completely on wire rack.

4. Fill each shell with about 3 tablespoons pudding; arrange fruit on top.

Makes 6 tarts

Strawberry Shake

1 cup sliced strawberries
1 cup vanilla or strawberry ice cream
1 cup cold milk

Place strawberries, ice cream and milk in blender; blend until smooth.

Makes 2 servings

Philadelphia® Classic Cheesecake

1½ cups HONEY MAID® Graham Cracker Crumbs
  3 tablespoons sugar
  ⅓ cup butter or margarine, melted
  4 packages (8 ounces each) PHILADELPHIA® Cream Cheese, softened
  1 cup sugar
  1 teaspoon vanilla
  4 eggs

1. Preheat oven to 325°F if using a silver 9-inch springform pan (or to 300°F if using a dark nonstick springform pan). Mix crumbs, 3 tablespoons sugar and butter; press firmly onto bottom of pan.

2. Beat cream cheese, 1 cup sugar and vanilla with electric mixer on medium speed until well blended. Add eggs, 1 at a time, mixing on low speed after each addition just until blended. Pour over crust.

3. Bake 55 minutes or until center is almost set. Loosen cake from side of pan; cool before removing side of pan. Refrigerate 4 hours or overnight. Store leftover cheesecake in refrigerator.   *Makes 16 servings*

Special Extra: Top with fresh fruit just before serving.

Prep Time: 20 minutes plus refrigerating • Bake Time: 55 minutes

Triple Chocolate Pudding Cake

1 cup biscuit baking mix
½ cup sugar
¼ cup unsweetened cocoa powder
¾ cup milk, divided
⅓ cup butter, softened
¾ cup hot fudge topping, divided
1 teaspoon vanilla
1 cup semisweet chocolate chips, divided
¾ cup coffee or hot water
    Whipped cream (optional)

1. Preheat oven to 350°F. Grease 8-inch square baking pan.

2. Combine baking mix, sugar and cocoa in medium bowl. Beat in ½ cup milk, butter, ¼ cup hot fudge topping and vanilla until well blended. Stir in ½ cup chocolate chips. Pour batter into prepared pan.

3. Combine remaining ¼ cup milk, ½ cup hot fudge topping and coffee in small bowl; stir until well blended. Pour over batter in pan. *Do not stir.* Sprinkle remaining ½ cup chocolate chips over top.

4. Bake 45 to 50 minutes or until set. Let stand 15 minutes on wire rack. Spoon pudding cake into dessert dishes. Serve with whipped cream, if desired.   *Makes 8 servings*

Strawberry Chocolate Chip Shortcake

1 cup sugar, divided
½ cup (1 stick) butter or margarine, softened
1 egg
2 teaspoons vanilla extract, divided
1½ cups all-purpose flour
½ teaspoon baking powder
1 cup HERSHEY'S Mini Chips Semi-Sweet Chocolate, HERSHEY'S SPECIAL DARK® Chocolate Chips or HERSHEY'S Semi-Sweet Chocolate Chips, divided
1 container (16 ounces) dairy sour cream
2 eggs
2 cups frozen non-dairy whipped topping, thawed
Fresh strawberries, rinsed and halved

1. Heat oven to 350°F. Grease 9-inch springform pan.

2. Beat ½ cup sugar and butter in large bowl. Add 1 egg and 1 teaspoon vanilla; beat until creamy. Gradually add flour and baking powder, beating until smooth; stir in ½ cup small chocolate chips. Press mixture onto bottom of prepared pan.

3. Stir together sour cream, remaining ½ cup sugar, 2 eggs and remaining 1 teaspoon vanilla in medium bowl; stir in remaining ½ cup small chocolate chips. Pour over mixture in pan.

4. Bake 50 to 55 minutes until almost set in center and edges are lightly browned. Cool completely on wire rack; remove side of pan. Spread whipped topping over top. Cover; refrigerate. Just before serving, arrange strawberry halves on top of cake; garnish as desired. Refrigerate leftover dessert. *Makes 12 servings*

Cupcake Sundaes

1 package (about 19 ounces) brownie mix, plus ingredients to
  prepare mix
Ice cream, any flavor
1 jar (8 ounces) hot fudge or caramel ice cream topping
  Colored sprinkles and chopped nuts (optional)
  Maraschino cherries

1. Preheat oven to 350°F. Spray 12 standard (2½-inch) muffin cups with nonstick cooking spray.

2. Prepare brownie mix according to package directions for cakelike brownies.* Spoon batter evenly into prepared muffin cups. Bake 20 to 25 minutes or until toothpick inserted into centers comes out clean. Cool cupcakes in pan on wire rack 5 minutes. Remove to rack; cool completely.

3. Cut off rounded tops of cupcakes; set aside. Place cupcakes on serving plates; top each with scoop of ice cream. Crumble reserved cupcake tops over sundaes. Drizzle with hot fudge topping; garnish with sprinkles and cherries.   *Makes 12 sundaes*

If package does not include directions for cakelike brownies, add one more egg than directions call for.

Sweet Potato Pie

1 pound sweet potatoes,* boiled and peeled
¼ cup (½ stick) butter or margarine
1 (14-ounce) can EAGLE BRAND® Sweetened Condensed Milk (NOT evaporated milk)
2 eggs
1 teaspoon grated orange rind
1 teaspoon vanilla extract
1 teaspoon ground cinnamon
1 teaspoon ground nutmeg
¼ teaspoon salt
1 (9-inch) unbaked pie crust

For best results, use fresh sweet potatoes.

1. Preheat oven to 350°F. In large bowl, beat sweet potatoes and butter until smooth. Add EAGLE BRAND®, eggs, orange rind, vanilla, cinnamon, nutmeg and salt; mix well. Pour into crust.

2. Bake 40 minutes or until golden brown. Cool. Garnish as desired. Store leftovers covered in refrigerator.   *Makes 1 (9-inch) pie*

Prep Time: 20 minutes • Bake Time: 40 minutes

When purchasing sweet potatoes, look for firm tubers with smooth, unbruised skin. Store sweet potatoes in a cool (55°F), dry, dark place. Properly stored, they may last up to 3 or 4 weeks, but it's best to use them as soon after purchase as possible.

Deep Dish Blueberry Pie

6 cups fresh blueberries *or* 2 (16-ounce) packages frozen
    blueberries, thawed
2 tablespoons lemon juice
1¼ cups sugar
3 tablespoons quick-cooking tapioca
¼ teaspoon ground cinnamon
1 tablespoon butter, cut into 4 pieces
1 package (15 ounces) refrigerated pie crusts

1. Preheat oven to 400°F.

2. Place blueberries in large bowl and sprinkle with lemon juice.
Combine sugar, tapioca and cinnamon in small bowl. Gently stir sugar
mixture into blueberries until blended.

3. Roll 1 crust into 12-inch circle on lightly floured work surface. Press
crust into 9-inch deep-dish pie pan. Trim all but ½ inch of overhang.
Spoon blueberry mixture over crust; dot top with butter pieces.

4. Roll remaining crust into 10-inch circle. Using small cookie cutter or
knife, cut 4 or 5 shapes from crust for vents. Place crust over blueberry
mixture. Trim edge, leaving 1-inch border. Fold edge under and even with
pan. Crimp edge with fork.

5. Bake 15 minutes. *Reduce heat to 350°F.* Bake 40 minutes or until
crust is browned and filling is bubbly. Cool on wire rack 30 minutes
before serving. *Makes 9 servings*

Triple-Layer Lemon Meringue Pie

2 cups cold milk
2 packages (4-serving size each) JELL-O® Lemon Flavor Instant
    Pudding & Pie Filling
1 tablespoon lemon juice
1 HONEY MAID® Graham Pie Crust (6 ounces)
1 tub (8 ounces) COOL WHIP® Whipped Topping, thawed, divided
2½ cups JET-PUFFED® Miniature Marshmallows, divided
2 tablespoons cold milk

1. Pour 2 cups milk into large bowl. Add dry pudding mixes and juice. Beat with wire whisk 2 minutes or until well blended. (Mixture will be thick.)

2. Spread 1½ cups of the pudding onto bottom of crust; set aside. Add half of the whipped topping to remaining pudding; stir gently until well blended. Spread over pudding layer in crust. Place 2 cups of the marshmallows in large microwaveable bowl. Add 2 tablespoons milk; stir. Microwave on High 1½ minutes or until marshmallows are completely melted, stirring after 1 minute. Stir until well blended. Refrigerate 15 minutes or until cooled. Gently stir in whipped topping; spread over pudding mixture.

3. Refrigerate 3 hours or until set. Top with the remaining ½ cup marshmallows just before serving. Store leftover pie in refrigerator.

Makes 8 servings, 1 slice each

Jazz It Up: Garnish with lemon twists or ½ cup sliced strawberries just before serving.

Prep Time: 15 minutes • **Total Time:** 3 hours 15 minutes (includes refrigerating)

Coconut Cream Pie

1½ cups sweetened shredded coconut
2 packages (4-serving size each) vanilla pudding and pie filling mix,
  plus ingredients to prepare mix
1 (6-ounce) graham cracker pie crust

1. Preheat oven to 350°F. Spread coconut on baking sheet. Toast coconut 10 minutes, stirring frequently; cool. Reserve 2 tablespoons coconut.

2. Prepare pudding according to package directions. Stir in remaining coconut.

3. Pour pudding mixture into pie crust. Sprinkle reserved coconut on top. Refrigerate 1 to 2 hours or until pudding is set.   *Makes 8 servings*

Low-Fat Chocolate-Banana Parfaits

2 cups cold fat free milk
1 package (4-serving size) JELL-O® Chocolate Flavor Fat Free Sugar
  Free Instant Reduced Calorie Pudding & Pie Filling
2 medium bananas, sliced
¾ cup thawed COOL WHIP® Sugar Free Whipped Topping, divided

1. Pour milk into medium bowl. Add dry pudding mix. Beat with wire whisk 2 minutes or until well blended.

2. Spoon half of the pudding evenly into 4 dessert glasses. Cover with layers of banana slices, ½ cup of the whipped topping and the remaining pudding. Top with remaining whipped topping.

3. Serve immediately. Or cover and refrigerate until ready to serve.
Makes 4 servings, 1 parfait each

Prep Time: 10 minutes • Total Time: 10 minutes

Caramel Apple Cheesecake

1 ¼ cups graham cracker crumbs
¼ cup (½ stick) butter, melted
3 packages (8 ounces each) cream cheese, softened
¾ cup sugar
1 ½ teaspoons vanilla
3 eggs
1 ¼ cups apple pie filling
½ cup chopped peanuts
¼ cup caramel ice cream topping

1. Preheat oven to 350°F. Spray 9-inch springform pan with nonstick cooking spray.

2. Combine graham cracker crumbs and butter in small bowl; press into bottom of prepared pan. Bake 9 minutes; cool on wire rack.

3. Beat cream cheese, sugar and vanilla in large bowl with electric mixer at medium speed until well blended. Add eggs; beat well. Pour cream cheese mixture over crust.

4. Bake 40 to 50 minutes or until center is almost set. Cool completely on wire rack. Refrigerate at least 3 hours. Carefully run knife around edge to loosen pan; remove side of pan.

5. Spread apple filling over top of cheesecake. Sprinkle peanuts over apple filling and drizzle with caramel topping. Serve immediately. Refrigerate leftovers.

Makes 12 servings

ACKNOWLEDGMENTS

The publisher would like to thank the companies and organizations listed below for the use of their recipes and photographs in this publication.

Campbell Soup Company

EAGLE BRAND®

The Hershey Company

©2010 Kraft Foods, KRAFT, KRAFT Hexagon Logo, PHILADELPHIA AND PHILADELPHIA Logo are registered trademarks of Kraft Foods Holdings, Inc. All rights reserved.

Nestlé USA

Ortega®, A Division of B&G Foods, Inc.

Recipes courtesy of the Reynolds Kitchens

Tyson Foods, Inc.

Unilever

Wisconsin Milk Marketing Board

VOLUME MEASUREMENTS (dry)

1/8 teaspoon = 0.5 mL
1/4 teaspoon = 1 mL
1/2 teaspoon = 2 mL
3/4 teaspoon = 4 mL
1 teaspoon = 5 mL
1 tablespoon = 15 mL
2 tablespoons = 30 mL
1/4 cup = 60 mL
1/3 cup = 75 mL
1/2 cup = 125 mL
2/3 cup = 150 mL
3/4 cup = 175 mL
1 cup = 250 mL
2 cups = 1 pint = 500 mL
3 cups = 750 mL
4 cups = 1 quart = 1 L

VOLUME MEASUREMENTS (fluid)

1 fluid ounce (2 tablespoons) = 30 mL
4 fluid ounces (1/2 cup) = 125 mL
8 fluid ounces (1 cup) = 250 mL
12 fluid ounces (1 1/2 cups) = 375 mL
16 fluid ounces (2 cups) = 500 mL

WEIGHTS (mass)

1/2 ounce = 15 g
1 ounce = 30 g
3 ounces = 90 g
4 ounces = 120 g
8 ounces = 225 g
10 ounces = 285 g
12 ounces = 360 g
16 ounces = 1 pound = 450 g

DIMENSIONS

1/16 inch = 2 mm
1/8 inch = 3 mm
1/4 inch = 6 mm
1/2 inch = 1.5 cm
3/4 inch = 2 cm
1 inch = 2.5 cm

OVEN TEMPERATURES

250°F = 120°C
275°F = 140°C
300°F = 150°C
325°F = 160°C
350°F = 180°C
375°F = 190°C
400°F = 200°C
425°F = 220°C
450°F = 230°C

BAKING PAN SIZES

Utensil	Size in Inches/Quarts	Metric Volume	Size in Centimeters
Baking or Cake Pan (square or rectangular)	8×8×2	2 L	20×20×5
	9×9×2	2.5 L	23×23×5
	12×8×2	3 L	30×20×5
	13×9×2	3.5 L	33×23×5
Loaf Pan	8×4×3	1.5 L	20×10×7
	9×5×3	2 L	23×13×7
Round Layer Cake Pan	8×1½	1.2 L	20×4
	9×1½	1.5 L	23×4
Pie Plate	8×1¼	750 mL	20×3
	9×1¼	1 L	23×3
Baking Dish or Casserole	1 quart	1 L	—
	1½ quart	1.5 L	—
	2 quart	2 L	—